P9-DNG-461

This Book is for

_____

NAME

Prepare for Your Soul to

A W A K E N

_____

DATE

A W A K E N

www.awakenhumanity.org

ERWIN RAPHAEL MCMANUS

STAND AGAINST THE WIND

AWAKEN THE HERO WITHIN

COUNTRYMAN

NASHVILLE, TENNESSEE

> *"Lord, if it's you," Peter replied,*
> *"tell me to come to you on the water." "Come," he said.*
> *Then Peter got down out of the boat,*
> *walked on the water and came toward Jesus.*
> But when he saw the wind, he was afraid
> *and, beginning to sink, cried out, "Lord, save me!"*

MATTHEW 14:28-30 NIV

The TRANSFORMATION of our character is more REVOLUTION than reformation. It is forged from battles fought far more than by beliefs held. It emerges out of crisis, not out of classroom. It doesn't just come to you; you must run to it. It is like a gauntlet waiting to be conquered. *Character is like a hero asleep within you waiting to be awakened.* Its power sweeps through you in waves of transformation. In pursuing a life that is not about yourself, you find yourself living *the life you've always longed for.* And with each challenge faced, with each victory won, you suddenly come to the realization that

you are a different person than the one who began the journey.
Simply attempting the gauntlet has changed you forever. Peter
saw the wind, was gripped by fear, and began to sink. But don't
miss the point—he stepped into the storm and walked on water!

Immediately Jesus reached out his hand and caught him.
"You of little faith," he said, "why did you doubt?"
And when they climbed into the boat, the wind died down.
Then those who were in the boat worshiped him, saying,
"Truly you are the Son of God."

MATTHEW 14:31-33 NIV

STAND AGAINST THE WIND

CHAPTER ONE

RUNNING FREE

It is for FREEDOM *that Christ has set us free.*
GALATIANS 5:1
NIV

You were created to be FREE.

If you are a follower of *Jesus Christ*,

you're also CALLED to be free.

Yet to experience this freedom,

there must first be an *uprising*—

a REVOLUTION of the soul.

This is how life is supposed to work—
it's an ADVENTURE, a JOURNEY, a trek filled with uncertainty,
excitement, and risk. I am convinced that in each of us there is
A VOICE CRYING OUT, a confession waiting to be declared
without shame, "I want to live!"
This journey requires many confessions and declarations, but
this is a good place to begin. Let me invite you to *hear the roar*
within your own soul.

God formed us in His image and then breathed life into us.
God's life in us is sustained by character. When we lose the character
of God, we lose the life of God in us. But to have His character,
we must first die to ourselves, because TO BECOME LIKE HIM
IS WHAT IT MEANS TO REALLY LIVE.

WE WERE CREATED WITH A PASSION TO LIVE.
When a man loses his will to live, he has essentially begun the
first stage of dying. So many of us have abdicated our passions
for obligations, as if passion is a luxury for the young and we all
must grow up one day.

Our incessant drive to eliminate sin has more than contributed
to the problem of passionless living.
We've believed that human passions are adversarial to God and
corrupting in their nature. We've been taught that God's solution
to restraining our passions is His commands. The result has been a
Christian religion based on RULES, RITUALS, and OBLIGATIONS.
When this becomes the case, Christianity as a religion is
essentially no different or better than the other major world
religions, all of which instruct followers to restrain their passions
to be better people. This is the essence of the Buddha—

to exist without desire.

2 CHRONICLES 15:15

The Scriptures place human DESIRES and

JOB 17:11

PASSIONS at *the epicenter of human*

PSALM 10:17-18

action. This is true in both the arena of sin and the arena of

PSALM 16:11

holiness. The goal of the Christian journey cannot be the

PSALM 20:4-5   PSALM 21:2-4

elimination of desire and passion, because the Scriptures teach

PSALM 37:4

that God created us in His image and part of this reflection of

PSALM 69:9

God is a heart designed for passionate living. It has NEVER

PSALM 112:8

been God's intention to move us toward apathetic living.

PSALM 119:32   PROVERBS 13:12

Rather than eliminate our passions, He intends to overwhelm

them with new passions. *The furnace of our passions is our*

|EREMIAH 32:40   EZEKIEL 11:19-21

character, and while evil character burns hot for destructive

EZEKIEL 36:26

passions that consume and destroy, the character of God

|OHN 10:10

ignites passion for what is good and true. Our QUEST

ROMANS 1:24-26

is to have God's character formed in us, so that His passions

EPHESIANS 3:19   COLOSSIANS 2:10

might *burn in us.*

I THESSALONIANS 3:8

Deeper than our instinct to live is our longing to be alive.
Aliveness is different from existence.

Human passion inflames within us desire. Our hearts crave the
FREEDOM OF PLEASURE and the PLEASURE OF FREEDOM.
What often eludes us is that *the two are not the same.*

There is something strangely elusive about freedom.

No matter what state we're in, it seems that freedom is to be
found elsewhere in a place or experience that we do not have.

The child can't wait to be a teenager.

The teenager can't wait to have a driver's license.

When we're in high school,

we can't wait until we're in college.

We can't wait to be free of our parents' rules

and try everything they warned us against.

We are free to choose our career paths,

but then we hate our jobs and dream instead

of other opportunities.

We are free to pursue our own success, pleasure, and ambition
without regard to the wellbeing of those around us.

We are now free to live any life we choose.

Yet the things we choose in our freedom soon hold us as
THIER PRISONERS.

An overwhelming number of us feel TRAPPED in the lives we've created. The irony is that we are the cruel tyrants who hold ourselves captive, and the tragedy of our imprisonment reaches into the deepest caverns of our souls. Our passion to be free both ignites us and betrays us, and more often than not leads us to be consumed by an unforgiving fire.

The very fire that burns within us can destroy us.

NOT ALL FREE ACTS LEAD TO FREEDOM.

The choices you freely make may cost you a life of genuine freedom. This is why the Bible talks about the human experience in terms of being slaves to sin. Sin creates the illusion of freedom; it fools us into seeking freedom from God rather than finding freedom in God.

Whatever else Jesus came to do, one thing is clear—He came to set you free. *God is not a warden; He is a deliverer.* And so earnest is He about your freedom that He was willing to be taken captive and crucified on your behalf just so you can run free.

FREEDOM IS THE GIFT OF SERVING OTHERS OUT OF L·IVE. This is the freedom that only God can give, where we once again become like Him. It is here and only here that freedom exists without boundaries. You are free to love without limit, to forgive, to be merciful, to be generous, to be compassionate, to risk, to sacrifice, to enjoy, and to live. . . . *And when you are free, you know it.*

When you make God your primary passion, He transforms all the passions of your heart. The result of this transformation is that it will be God's pleasure to fulfill those passions. *When God is your desire, you can trust the passions of your heart.* In this state you can most fully live a uniquely passionate life.

IT IS NOT INCIDENTAL
THAT THE DEATH OF JESUS IS CALLED
THE PASSI·N.

Living is no low-risk proposition. IF LIFE IS AN ADVENTURE, THEN *danger is inherent to the journey.* How often have we surrendered our freedoms under the weight of our fears? This is one of the main reasons we abdicate living for existing. As mundane as it is, *existing provides a level of predictability and safety.* Freedom is wild and wide-open, filled with uncharted territory.

I run in the path of your commands, for you have set my heart free.
—PSALM 119:32 NIV

Delight yourself in the LORD
and He will give you the desires of your heart.
—PSALM 37:4 NIV

David unlocks for us the real essence of freedom. Because God has set his heart free, he can pursue a life of truth. WE ARE FINALLY FREE TO BE ALIVE ONLY WHEN GOD FREES OUR HEARTS FROM THE PASSIONS THAT IMPRISON US.

OUR CAPACITY TO RUN FREE IS RELATED TO OUR COMMITMENT TO STAND FIRM. There is a discipline of the heart that marks the free spirit. All of us long to play the song in our souls, and more of us would do so if it didn't require endless hours of studying the notes.

Do not conform any longer to the pattern of this world, but be transformed by the renewing of your mind. Then you will be able to test and approve what God's will is—his good, pleasing, and perfect will.
ROMANS 12:2 NIV

If anyone is in Christ, he is a new creation; the old has gone, the new has come!
2 CORINTHIANS 5:17 NIV

Everyone who desires a revolution of the soul must first heed their tired, tattered soul cry: **"I want to change!"** YOU CAN'T ESCAPE WHO YOU ARE. You will be forever stuck inside your skin. BUT YOU CAN BECOME SOMEONE ELSE. You can leave behind the person you've grown to despise and become a person who even you can admire. *This transformation requires no one less than Jesus Christ.*

IF YOU WANT TO RUN FREE, you must first *see the counterfeit* that holds and molds you to the pattern of this world. Second, you must KNOW THE WAY through the character matrix. To want godly character is one thing; to know how to acquire it is another. The path is revealed by Jesus Christ. To choose His way is to cast away the false and find true liberation. An uprising—A REVOLUTION OF THE SOUL—awaits you. If you choose to break free, you will stand apart from the masses. At times you will stand alone. But if you are willing to risk everything, you will find two forces that will change your life forever—God and yourself!

CHAPTER TWO

THE DROWNING POOL

At one time you were separated from God. . . .

But now God has made you his friends again . . .

as people who are holy, with no wrong, and with

nothing of which God can judge you guilty.

COLOSSIANS 1:21-22 NCV

To discover
what it means to be
TRULY HUMAN,
the *only one* we can
turn to is GOD.

Narcissus is perhaps the best candidate to serve as humanity's patron saint. In the Greek myth, he was the image of perfection. His offers of love seemed endless, but he rejected them all as unworthy. Then one day Narcissus stooped to drink from a clear, shaded pool. There *he finally fell in love* ⋯ with his own reflection. He pined away on the shore, longing for nothing more than his own image. His self-love paralyzed him, *leaving him at the drowning pool* and costing him a life of divine quality.

When we are in love with ourselves, we are prone to listen only to what we want to hear. We become more than willing to trade insight for affirmation. *We want to* FEEL GOOD *about ourselves more than we want ourselves to* BECOME GOOD.

Jesus commends and even commands an aspect of self-love, yet there is a difference between loving ourselves and being in love with ourselves. The first rests our value in God; the second demands a value above all others. When we value ourselves properly, we do not devalue others. When we devalue ourselves, we deny our divine value. When we treat others as immeasurably valuable, we ourselves become invaluable. Loving ourselves is the natural result of yielding ourselves to the selfless love of God.

In selfless love we find ourselves full and fulfilled. Self-love voraciously feeds itself and destines us to live in the vacuum of an empty center.

PROVERBS 1:7

PROVERBS 14:7-9

PROVERBS 18:6-7

PROVERBS 18:2

When we choose to live a life of "self,"
we become what the ancients called a fool.

PROVERBS 3:35

PROVERBS 1:7

PROVERBS 29:11

PROVERBS 26:3-12

OUR NEED TO BE LOVED AND VALUED is placed within us by God and ultimately can be fulfilled only by Him. Our insecurities and our sinfulness have led us to take this assignment on for ourselves. When our lives are defined by self-love, we not only make ourselves unlovely, but at the same time we diminish our capacity to experience and give love.

Let nothing be done through SELFISH *ambition or conceit, but in lowliness of mind let each esteem others better than himself. Let each of you look out not only for his own interests, but also for the interests of others. Let this mind be in you which was also in Christ Jesus, who, being in the form of God, did not consider it robbery to be equal with God, but made Himself of no reputation, taking the form of a bondservant, and coming in the likeness of men. And being found in appearance as a man, He humbled Himself and became obedient to the point of death, even the death of the cross. Therefore God also has highly exalted Him and given Him the name which is above every name, that at the name of Jesus every knee should bow, of those in heaven, and of those on earth, and of those under the earth, and that every tongue should confess that Jesus Christ is Lord, to the glory of God the Father.*

PHILIPPIANS 2:3-11 NKJV

While the journey is filled with promise of all that is to come, our quest begins first with what we must relinquish. We are instructed to do nothing out of selfish ambition (greed) or vain conceit (pride). When we live life fueled by these motives, we choose the life of a fool. AMBITION ITSELF IS NOT WRONG. In fact, the Bible never speaks of ambition itself as negative. Ambition is not the problem; IT'S SELFISH AMBITION FROM WHICH WE NEED TO BE FREED. But we've been better at destroying ambition than at eliminating selfishness.

THE MORE SELF-ORIENTED WE ARE, THE MORE CONTROLLING WE ARE. But some things are simply out of our hands. When God is not a part of our lives, we tend to act as if we are God. Many of us are willing to settle for the feeling of being in control rather than making the choices that genuinely will give us freedom. While we strive to fill ourselves and remain empty, Jesus emptied Himself and lived fully. The road Jesus walked was not an easy one. Rather than safety and comfort, He promises adventure and risk. *He offers the way to true greatness.* He promises that if we will follow Him, we will become like Him at journey's end.

YOU CANNOT FOLLOW JESUS AND REMAIN THE SAME. The journey itself will change you forever—not only your priorities but your passions. It alters not only your direction but your desires. It transforms not only your actions but your values. It makes you just like Christ and unlike anyone else. *It is nothing less than leaving the fake for the real.* There is great risk in abandoning the artificial in pursuit of the authentic. Yet if we've never known the real thing, it's easy to understand why we are mesmerized with the best versions of the imitations.

"Therefore whoever hears these sayings of Mine, and does them, I will liken him to A WISE MAN who built his house on the rock: and the rain descended, the floods came, AND THE WINDS BLEW and beat on that house; AND IT DID NOT FALL, for it was founded on the rock.

"But everyone who hears these sayings of Mine, and does not do them, will be like A FOOLISH MAN who built his house on the sand: and the rain descended, the floods came, AND THE WINDS BLEW and beat on that house; AND IT FELL. And great was its fall."

MATTHEW 7:24-27 NKJV

TO DISCOVER WHAT IT MEANS TO BE TRULY HUMAN, the only one we can turn to is God. It's not that the fool doesn't know what to do; he just chooses to ignore the voice of God. *A person God Himself deems as wise is one who not only hears His voice, but immediately begins to act upon His instruction.*

CHAPTER THREE

RISING OUT OF THE ASHES

God has chosen you and made you his holy people. He loves you.

So always do these things: Show mercy to others, be kind, humble,

gentle, and patient. Get along with each other, and forgive each other.

. . . love each other. . . . Let the peace that Christ gives control your

thinking . . . Always be thankful.

COLOSSIANS 3:12-15 NCV

HUMILITY

is coming to grips with our

humanity. Our humility

allows GOD'S INTERVENTION.

Neither perspective nor attitude is formed in a vacuum. They are expressions of deeper realities within us. WHEN A PERSON HAS AN ATTITUDE PROBLEM, WHAT HE OR SHE REALLY HAS IS AN ARROGANCE PROBLEM.

A bad attitude is evidence of a lack of humility. Attitude is an accurate monitor of where we fall on the spectrum of pride and humility. This is why two people can step into the same experience and respond to it so differently. It's why sometimes we need an attitude adjustment. *Violence is arrogance when it doesn't get its way.*

When we are most FULL OF OURSELVES, we are most likely to make FOOLS OF OURSELVES. And when we are full of ourselves we leave no room for God to place in us the very things we need the most. *Pride fills up the space where integrity needs to reside.*

COURAGE IS THE STRENGTH OF HEART
BORN OUT OF INTEGRITY.

A PERSON OF INTEGRITY IS A PERSON OF TRUTH.
Yet truth itself is not what *forms* integrity; rather, it's what
informs integrity. Only the teachable heart will embrace whatever
truth is needed for the moment. If we are not teachable, there
will be no transformation. If we are unwilling to listen, we are
incapable of learning. That is why Jesus calls us to be disciples
and to make disciples. *It is the student of life who will learn
how to live.* And while intelligence, discipline, focus, and
determination are all critical to the learning process, another
characteristic is even more essential: humility.

INTEGRITY IS FORMED IN THE HEART OF THE HUMBLE.
The quest for honor leads us to courage through integrity and to
integrity through humility. There is no other path. If you desire
the kind of greatness that not only inspires admiration of others
but also leads to genuine friendships and true intimacy, then
only the way of humility will do. *If all you care about is
yourself, that's all you're going to have.*

GOD IS NOT IMPRESSED WITH TALENT NEARLY AS MUCH AS HE IS WITH CHARACTER. Humility, gratitude, and faithfulness are the critical triad if we are to walk in the steps of Jesus. Moses was exactly what Pharaoh was not. By choosing the path of humility, Moses began a divine odyssey that forever would mark human history.

GOD'S PURPOSE MUST ALWAYS BE FULFILLED IN LINE WITH GOD'S CHARACTER.

How do you move toward humility without losing it in the pursuit? *Humility begins with self-awareness, and that must be followed with selflessness.* If God gives grace to the humble, that's where I want to be.

GOD IN HIS NATURE IS HUMBLE. Without humility a God of infinite power would use His resources to impress rather than to transform. Without humility God would find no value in us, nor would He be concerned for our wellbeing. The realization that God, in all of His power and knowledge and wonder, is more humble than any of us is virtually beyond comprehension.

In your lives you must think and act like Christ Jesus.
Christ himself was like God in everything. But he did not think that
being equal with God was something to be used for his own benefit.
But he gave up his place with God and made himself nothing.
He was born to be a man and became like a servant.
And when he was living as a man,
he humbled himself and was fully obedient to God,
even when that caused his death—death on a cross.

PHILIPPIANS 2:5-8 NCV

Had Jesus come with power and royalty, wealth and prestige, it
would have approved all the things we lust after. Had He chosen
the path that pointed to the highest treasures of men, it would
have led us away from the treasures of God. Instead, Jesus was
most honored because He was most humble. He has been
exalted to the highest place for He alone was willing to go to
the lowest place.

GOD IS HOLY AND IN HIS HOLINESS HE CHOOSES
TO DWELL AMONG THE HUMBLE.

HUMILITY BRINGS US TO GOD NOT OUT OF OBLIGATION BUT OUT OF GRATITUDE. When we humble ourselves we choose the place of least honor and allow God to call us to any role of servanthood He might desire. Humility begins with emptying ourselves so that we can receive from God all that we need for the journey.

We are never called in the Bible to pray for humility; instead we are commanded to be humble. There are some things that GOD DOES and some things GOD REQUIRES. While humility is a divine attribute, it is placed squarely on our shoulders to **choose** this path. When we refuse to humble ourselves and God has to insist on it, the experience is more than humbling; it is humiliating.

We cannot enter into a genuine relationship with God without coming to Him in humility. *Repentance requires humility, and humility is most practically expressed in submission.*

When we submit ourselves to God, we are placing our lives under His mission. Submission is not about powerlessness; it is about meekness. TO BE MEEK IS TO HAVE CONTROLLED STRENGTH. Like the Roman centurion (Matthew 8:5-13) we must be people both *of* authority and *under* authority.

We cannot be entrusted with authority over others if we cannot be trusted to live under the authority of others. That's one reason why children who are never taught to honor and submit to their parents make such poor adults. HUMILITY GIVES US THE MOBILITY TO ADAPT TO WHATEVER CONTEXT WE ENCOUNTER.

Anywhere God walks is not beneath us. In Jesus we see that the power of God is unleashed to accomplish His greatest good when we are willing to walk in humility.

TO BE HUMBLE IS TO BE TRULY GREAT.

CHAPTER FOUR

CREATING OUT OF THE PIECES

And you will joyfully give thanks to the Father who has made you able to have a share in all that he has prepared for his people in the kingdom of light.

COLOSSIANS 1:12 NCV

When we are GRATEFUL, we are most *fully alive.* Gratitude allows us to absorb every possible pleasure from a moment.

THE OPPOSITE OF GREED IS NOT POVERTY, BUT GENEROSITY. While it is no small challenge to learn how to live without, it is an even greater challenge to learn to live with. The pursuit of poverty is an abdication of responsibility. Although we must not just live for ourselves, at the same time we must not be afraid to enjoy what God has given us. God entrusts people with resources not so we will hoard or ignore them, but so we will use them for the good and enjoyment of others. Too many of us neglect the good WE COULD DO to avoid the evil WE MIGHT DO. The solution is not to stop doing good in order to ensure that we don't do evil. *God frees us from sin not to leave us empty but to fill us with life.* His goal is not to replace sin with inaction. You don't fill a vacuum with a vacuum. *You overcome selfishness with servanthood and greed with generosity.* As tempting as it may be to live detached from the world around us, it is not in keeping with the heart of God.

It is so easy to confuse Christianity with Buddhism in this way. We know that greed corrupts and destroys, so we conclude that the only way to be free is to detach ourselves from all human desire until we withdraw ourselves from the world in which we live. Jesus, on the other hand, clearly enjoyed the life He lived. He was chastised for not living a monastic existence. *Jesus was having way too much fun* for the religious observers who watched Him. When we replace greed with generosity, we exchange a black hole for a wellspring. *The goal is not to have less, but to give more.* Generosity is the result of a life in continuous overflow.

God is the ultimate expression of wholeness. The dilemma in our pursuit of wholeness is that *brokenness is often laced with ungratefulness. Nothing will heal us if we are ungrateful.* Gratitude is central to the entire experience and journey of the Christian faith. *"Gratitude" and "grace"* share the same etymology and root. A life of gratitude makes us WH◍LE, overwhelms us with L◍VE, and moves us to LIVE generous lives.

Forgiveness unlocks gratitude, and gratitude unleashes love. *Forgiveness and gratitude are inseparable.* When we receive forgiveness, we grow in gratefulness. Our ability to receive forgiveness is directly related to our willingness to give it (Colossians 3:13-14). When we are grateful, we forgive freely. When we are grateful, we are not bound to grudges or vengeance. GRATITUDE *enables us to be generous with love.*

In the same way that gratitude is intertwined with forgiveness, *brokenness often is perpetuated by bitterness.* You cannot remain embittered and find wholeness (Ephesians 4:31-32). When someone desires forgiveness, it is your gift to give out of the generosity of your spirit. Even if someone does not desire your forgiveness, it is critical to *be free from the bitterness that will enslave you.*

Gratitude and forgiveness are inseparable, as are ungratefulness and bitterness. When we are grateful, we experience life with a healthy optimism. When we lack gratitude, we move toward pessimism. *An ungrateful heart always sees what's wrong with life.* The longer we live without gratitude, the more embittered we become.

Bitterness creates an illusion of control and power.
It is an attempt to hold someone prisoner to an experience or action in the past, but the reality is that our bitterness traps no one but ourselves.

GRATITUDE FUELS OPTIMISM AND INSPIRES HOPE.
The quality of hope can only exist in relationship to the future (Romans 8:24-25). When hope is directed toward the past, it becomes despair. *Hope can only exist in the future.* This is one reason why embittered people ultimately cannot be encouraged into a new frame of thinking. Until they're willing to let go of the past, they are not ready to take hold of the future.

Grace both receives and gives forgiveness without measure. To receive the grace of God and yet treat others ungraciously is an act of wickedness. God's expectation is that we get rid of all bitterness, rage, brawling, slander, and malice and "be kind and compassionate to one another, forgiving each other, just as in Christ God forgave [us]" (Ephesians 4:32 NIV).

BITTERNESS ALWAYS FEELS JUSTIFIED.
Instead of bitterness, Jesus chose forgiveness. He calls us to do the same not only for the sake of others but for the salvation of our own souls. *When we are free from bitterness, we are free to pursue the life God dreams for us.*

Try to live in peace with all people, and try to live free from sin. Anyone whose life is not holy will never see the Lord. Be careful that no one fails to receive God's grace and begins to cause trouble among you. A person like that can ruin many of you.
HEBREWS 12:14-15 NCV

WHEN WE EMBRACE BITTERNESS, WE REJECT GRACE. Bitterness destroys our relationships, impairs our judgment, skews our perspective, and distorts our memories.

Gratitude generates optimism. The grace of God not only frees us from sin but from pessimism. When you trust God with your future, hope naturally abounds. *Gratitude changes your perspective about life.* You see the future, experience the present, and remember the past in a dramatically different way.

Remember the good and the good will grow.

When we realize that life is a gift and we are overwhelmed with a sense of gratitude, when we fill every moment with praise for God's goodness and thanks for His generosity . . .

. . . we find wholeness, and our hearts increase in their capacity to experience and give love.

CHAPTER FIVE

COMING OUT OF NOWHERE

Be joyful because you have hope.

Be patient when trouble comes,

and pray at all times.

ROMANS 12:12 NCV

God *desires* for us to become faithful, trustworthy people. PERSEVERANCE is the ability to remain faithful for the duration.

The quest for enlightenment leads us to the wisdom of God.
WISDEM IS FORGED THROUGH THE CRUCIBLE OF PERSEVERANCE.

If Rome wasn't built in a day, neither is character formed in one moment. There is a process in our becoming all that God created us to be. This is the human side of divine change. *Transformation is both the miracle of God and the stewardship of man.* Godliness is a result of both divine activity and human action. God promises to do what we cannot do for ourselves, and He commands us to do that which He will not do for us. *There is both miracle and responsibility.* God entrusts us with His resources, and then He holds us accountable for what we do with them.

It isn't very difficult to see that we are not all the same. Some people seem to have gotten an overload when God was handing out talents; others seem less gifted. But be assured *there is divine talent in you.* It is both waiting to be unleashed and depending on your being a faithful steward with what you've been entrusted. While we may be unable to perceive it, the great things of God come out of the small acts of faithfulness. When He finds we can be trusted with small things, we then are given responsibility over bigger things. *How we serve exposes how we would lead.*

When we are FAITHFUL, we are TRUSTWORTHY. The person who is unfaithful cannot be trusted. These two characteristics are inseparable.

If a person does not achieve his or her God-given potential, although we might consider it a tragedy we would never think of it as wickedness. But perhaps we should. After all, the servant in the parable of the talents was declared wicked when what he could have done was measured against what he did (Matthew 25:14-30).

There is a difference between the fear of God and being afraid of God. THE FEAR OF GOD SETS US FREE TO LIVE. Being afraid of God paralyzes us and reduces us to existing, not really living. A wrong view of God can lead us to lose both the potential of or lives and the pleasure of our God.

God sees not only who we are, but who we can become. *When we neglect our God-given capacity, when we refuse to maximize our God-given potential, it is wickedness in the sight of God.* How would it change the work of the church if our measure of effectiveness was not how little sin was being done, but how much good was being accomplished? A life lived against God is wickedness, and a life lived beneath our divine capacity is equally dishonoring to God.

You were created for more than just existing. While we have redefined mediocrity as normal and far too often expect nothing more than that from ourselves, God will not accept it. He did not create us to be average but to be unique. Only God really knows the person you were intended to become. Only He sees the full measure of what is neglected or lost.

Sin is what happens when we have too much time on our hands and too little purpose in our lives. *Sin fills a vacuum that is not supposed to be empty.* To give our lives to the elimination of sin is like trying to fill a black hole. The Bible tells us that the reward of sin is death (Romans 6:23). *Sin and life cannot coexist.* They are darkness and light.

Jesus reminds us that He came to give us life abundant (John 10:10). When you begin to live, sin falls off like pounds in a sauna. Some of the more difficult sins only come off when you run the treadmill, but when you begin to truly live you become free from sin. The vacuum is filled with life. The outcome is stewardship, and all of us have gifts for which God demands our stewardship. You have not been left empty-handed. To say you don't have talent is to contradict God.

Every one of us has God-given talent. We're all unique in the contributions we can make. All of us are complex and represent a composite of intelligence, passions, personality, skills, and talents. The dynamic interaction of all of these are the material from which we draw our potential. Potential is a glimpse of what could be, yet *there must be a shift from where we have* POTENTIAL *to where we are* POTENT.

Potential and productivity are not the same. You're not supposed to die with your potential. A life well-lived squeezes all the potential placed within and does something with it. *When potential is harnessed, we become potent.* Potential, when it becomes potent, always produces results. We are born with potential, but we are called to live productive lives. The fool squanders his potential. He is not faithful with what God has given him.

Those who are most faithful with the most resources will find expanding roles in God's kingdom. If God can help more people by entrusting you with far more than He gives to me, He will. It's not about how much you or I get; *it's about what we will do with what we have* (Luke 19).

When we are unfaithful, we are a bad investment. We may find ourselves blaming others for our failures, but in the end it's all us. When we are trustworthy, we can be entrusted with power. When we are faithful, our influence in the lives of others naturally will expand.

TALENT WITHOUT CHARACTER IS A DANGEROUS THING. TALENT FUELED BY CHARACTER IS A GIFT FROM GOD.

Character is formed in the crucible of faithfulness and refined through the gauntlet of perseverance. *The shape of your character is the shape of your future.*

We tend to seek wisdom only when we face an overwhelming crisis, and thus we miss an important truth: *there is wisdom in the small things,* the small choices. The seemingly minor decisions require wisdom just as much as the monumental ones. In fact, we find ourselves in so many crises because we failed to seek wisdom sooner. When we're entrusted with something, whether great or small, it is not inconsequential.

The implications of faithfulness cannot be overestimated and must not be underestimated.

When we work hard, our talents begin to be harnessed. Sometimes we will be called to serve outside of our most significant abilities, but even then the effect can be both positive and substantial.

Developing our talents is critical to maximizing our life impact; yet more important than this is the development of our character. *Faithfulness is about making significant those tasks entrusted to you that further the common good.* How you handle little decisions today will be the same way you'll act in your greatest moments of decision.

PERSEVERANCE IS THE FRUIT OF FAITHFULNESS.
FAITHFULNESS ACCELERATES WISDOM.

Whenever we are faithful with little, when we are trustworthy in the small matters, we accelerate our journey to wisdom. *Faithfulness by its very essence implies time.* Faith you can have in a moment; faithfulness takes a bit longer.

Jesus doesn't say we need to have *more* faith; He tells us we just need to have *some* (Matthew 17:20). It is not our faith in an event that is critical, but our faith in God Himself. It is not about believing in a miracle or believing for a miracle; it is about an *unshakable confidence in the character of God.*

Read Matthew 11:4-6. Why would anyone be tempted to fall away from a God who works so miraculously? Because although God can do all that was described, He is also the God who calls us to the greatest level of sacrifice. There are moments when our greatest act of faith is to remain faithful. FAITH IS NOT ALWAYS A WAY OUT OF CRISIS—in fact, it rarely is— but faith gives us the strength and confidence to see every challenge and crisis through to the end. Faith is a confidence in God that results in faithfulness. That faithfulness gives us the power to persevere.

For Jesus, wisdom wasn't just a download from heaven. When He became a man, He didn't cheat. He gained wisdom through the same process that we are invited to employ. He knew what to say because morning by morning He opened His ears and heart and became a student. *The wisdom of God comes to those who walk with God.* And the path is neither easy nor safe. It's difficult to think of Jesus as having to gain wisdom. We tend to think of Jesus as always complete in every way. To see this clearly, we only need to remember that

Jesus came into this world as an infant. He had to learn everything from scratch—how to eat, how to walk, how to speak, how to read, how to live.

No one journeys the path to wisdom without significant obstacles and hardship. We will all face the temptation to rebel or perhaps draw back, yet if we hold fast we will find the light of day. God loves to entrust even more to men and women who are faithful with what we have.

Faithfulness keeps your character from going bad. The small things don't seem very important in the moment, but they have huge ramifications in the future. It's not the great challenges that cause successful leaders to fall; it is the ignoring of the small things. When it comes to character the details really do matter. In your quest for honor, you have to sweat the small stuff. Great leaders in a very real way come out of nowhere. *We must never underestimate the weightiness of small matters.*

CHAPTER SIX

THE UNIFYING POWER OF BELIEVING

As for me, You uphold me in my integrity,

And set me before Your face forever.

PSALM 41:12 NKJV

INTEGRITY

is when the

heart of God is

joined with

the *heart of man*.

You can't say two different things at the same time and expect to be trusted. A person of integrity cannot say one thing and do another.

Integrity is the context from which courage is formed. Integrity, like wholeness, is a byproduct of our spiritual integration. "Integrity" comes from the root word "integer," which means to be complete, indivisible—in other words, to be whole.

In our culture we have put an increasing value on authenticity and a decreasing focus on integrity. We have disdain for the pretentious and we long for anything that is real. But we **mustn't romanticize authenticity.** When calling for authenticity, we need to take seriously the brokenness of the human heart. If we're not careful, *authentic* can be the new word for *arrogance*. As long as you're true to yourself how can anyone fault you, right? *Authenticity can establish a self-righteousness that justifies abuse.*

If we are committed to being the genuine article, first we'd better look closely at what we're made of. *Authenticity without integrity is lethal.*

To be authentic when our hearts are dark is equivalent to opening Pandora's box. As much as we disdain the external constraints of society, humanity's best solution without God is to establish laws that restrain the evil that lurks within us.

To be authentic means literally that we are not false or copied, that we reflect the original. Our separation from God has made us into imitations, no longer reflections of the Creator. Although we are born of a template designed in the image of the Creator God, that template is broken, and the reproduction flawed. WE ARE CLASSIC COUNTERFEITS. We pass as the real thing. We might even fool ourselves. Yet the evidence of our inauthenticity can be seen in our departure from the character of God. The first and most important step in becoming genuinely authentic is once again to *be authenticated by the original designer.* God longs to place within each of us a new heart, that reflects Him in both action and desire (EZEKIEL 36:26).

The divine transformation that God seeks to bring is nothing less and nothing more than making us fully human.

While religion works to restrain our actions from the outside in, **God always works from the inside out.** Only this kind of change lasts. It is in this state that we become people of integrity. It's more than "what you see is what you get." Integrity is not just about who we are, but who we seek to become. *Integrity is not about being flawless but being "falseless."*

EVERYTHING GOD CREATES HAS INTEGRITY.

With integrity comes integration. We align what others see with who we really are becoming. And more important, we align who we really are with who God is. When Jesus prayed for His disciples that they would be one as He and the Father are one (John 17), the focus of His prayer was unity. *Only in oneness with God do we find wholeness and integration.*

God created everything to be in proper relationship with Himself. Integrity is born out of relationship with God and flows into our relationships with others. *Integrity is the personification of truth.*

JESUS HAD ONLY ONE FACE. When we lack integrity, we find ourselves with several faces, being several people, depending on the circumstances. We become personality salesmen rather than people of substance. But Jesus was always the same person (Mark 12:14), and this is exactly what God both desires and requires of us. This same type of integrity is to be formed in us to shape our lives. As with Jesus, integrity is best showcased in the context of opposition or even persecution. When we face a moment of truth, our integrity is tested and proven genuine or not. In Jesus' three years of ministry, His environment grew in hostility, and every decision of integrity increased its volatility. That Jesus walked in integrity at all times, even when it cost Him His life, was the ultimate proof of who He was.

When we are defined by integrity, we respond with moral courage. COURAGE IS THE ULTIMATE EXPRESSION OF INTEGRITY. Integrity gives us the courage to walk in truth even when it means walking straight into the mouth of the dragon.

When we lack integrity, we live in fear (Proverbs 10:9, 28:1). We're afraid of getting caught, of someone knowing who we really are, but when we walk in righteousness and love what is right we have nothing to fear at all.

As we grow in integrity, we grow in the courage to live lives of conviction. The only actions we consider are those that reflect the character of God. *Integrity increases our capacity to live and act in a genuinely heroic way.* When Saul questioned whether David was up to the challenge of Goliath, David's response was a summary of his resume as a shepherd (1 Samuel 17:34-37). His response is *not a moment of inspiration, but a pattern of integrity.* The courage to face lions, bears, and giants was the outflow of the integrity of his heart.

The seriousness with which David took
his responsibility as a shepherd was the best
indicator for how he would respond if
entrusted with responsibility over God's people
(Psalm 78:70-72).

WHEN WE FEAR GOD, WE FEAR NOTHING ELSE.

We are free from all the fears that haunt
our hearts apart from God. The fear of God
aligns us with all that is true and good,
and it transforms the core motivation
of our hearts to become love.

INTEGRITY, OR THE LACK OF IT, HAS EVERYTHING TO DO WITH
HOW WE USE POWER.

The adage "Absolute power corrupts absolutely" is wrong. The only one who has ever known absolute power is God, and He is also the only one who has never abused power. The end result of absolute power motivated by undiluted love is SERVANTHOOD. Jesus' first act after knowing that all power had been placed under His authority was to wrap a towel around His waist and wash His disciples' feet (John 13:1-17).

Absolute power does not corrupt; it reveals.
Jesus is our proof of this.

Corruption is not an issue of power; it is an issue of passion. *Power allows us to unleash our passions.*

Character is the mark that defines who we really are when we get to the core. When our character is defined by integrity, we can be trusted with power. Power does not become a corrosive agent but a creative energy. When we lack integrity, we use power to control. *When we lead with integrity, we use power to bless.*

How Jesus used His authority was an extension of His use of power. With His power He served; with His authority he authorized; with His place of authority He chose not to hold power but to release it. After declaring His authority in heaven and earth He commissioned His disciples to act in His name. (Matthew 28:18-20).

Instead of hoarding His power, Jesus unleashes His power. For Him, neither love nor power is a limited commodity. *Just like love, the nature of power expands when it is given away.*

Power is a tool. It allows us the freedom to be who we truly are. This is why *it is critical to pursue integrity rather than power.* When you are promoted based on your abilities, without regard to the content of your character, it is a disservice both to your subordinates and to you. We do no one a favor when we put abilities over integrity.

Integrity cannot be gained by power and authority. Integrity must be gained long before these have been placed in our hands. Jesus lived an obscure life for thirty years preparing for a public ministry that lasted for only three.

Integrity requires that you decide what kind of person you want to become. *Integrity not only harnesses our passions but focuses our intentions.* Our course is guided by an internal compass of convictions fueled by passions.

The real measure of our power is the freedom and opportunity we create for others. Men and women who are marked by integrity point the way to freedom.

Perhaps the most amazing thing about integrity is when you still choose to do what's right when you're all alone, no one sees you, and no one will know what you do. *It's wonderful when you look inside your own heart and like what you see.*

CHAPTER SEVEN

THE HEALING POWER OF BELONGING

Love and truth belong to God's people;

goodness and peace will be theirs.

PSALM 85:10 NCV

We all need to be *loved*.
We all need *compassion*.
We all need *forgiveness*.
We all need *acceptance*.
And this is why, above all else,
we need GOD.

In the midst of our growing fragmentation, we have never been more focused on the individual than we are today. This focus plays itself out in unbridled consumerism. CONSUMERISM'S PRIMARY PRODUCT IN OUR CULTURE IS NARCISSISM. Even the language of pop psychology betrays us. "You can't love anyone else until you love yourself," is the mantra we are invited to embrace. We are given professional permission to put ourselves above everyone and everything else. "You've got to take what you need before you can give."

When we are broken, there's never enough.

When we are emotionally fragmented, we leak. No matter how much we consume, how much we take for ourselves, we always find ourselves empty in the end. This in turn leaves us only more frustrated and embittered. Our desperate search for wholeness requires us to let go of what we so long to take hold of and instead to set forth on a pilgrimage that leads along an entirely different path. *Wholeness is not found through receiving, but through giving.*

Wholeness and generosity are inseparably linked.

While it is true you cannot give what you do not have, you can give what you have not experienced. You can serve even if you've never been served. You can forgive even if you've never been forgiven. You can express compassion even if you've never received compassion. Generosity is not contingent on what you've received but on what you're willing to give.

To be truly generous, we must be generative. If we only give what we have received, we are nothing more than relational and emotional barterers.

"O divine Master, grant that I may not so much seek to be consoled as to console; to be understood as to understand; to be loved as to love. For it is in giving that we receive; it is in pardoning that we are pardoned; and it is in dying that we are born to eternal life."
ST. FRANCIS OF ASSISI (1182-1226)

Generosity in its primal essence is love. When we are broken, we become an emotional black hole. No matter how much is poured into us, its light is absorbed and never finds its way back out. When we are whole, we are nurtured by what is invested in us, and at the same time we freely give of ourselves to others.

When a person is whole, he or she sees love as limitless. We were designed to be CONDUITS OF LOVE; *the problem is we've been disconnected with the Source of love.*

We love because God first loved us (1 John 4:19). Love is so central to who God is that it is a primary test of our own relationship to the Creator (1 John 4:7-8).

The Scriptures describe us as being perfect and complete in this life (1 John 4:16-18; Ephesians 4:13). The best parallel word would be "wholeness." *The promise of God is not that we will be flawless in this world, but that we can be whole in this life.* We have wasted too much effort trying to become perfect in our actions and invested too little energy in becoming healthy in our spirits. God intended us literally to generate love—*we were designed specifically to be love machines.*

May the Lord make your love grow more and multiply for each other and for all people so that you will love others as we love you.

1 THESSALONIANS 3:12 NCV

This is my prayer for you: that your love will grow more and more; that you will have knowledge and understanding with your love; that you will see the difference between good and bad and will choose the good; that you will be pure and without wrong for the coming of Christ; that you will do many good things with the help of Christ to bring glory and praise to God.

PHILIPPIANS 1:9-11 NCV

I ask the Father in his great glory to give you the power to be strong inwardly through his Spirit. I pray that Christ will live in your hearts by faith and that your life will be strong in love and be built on love. And I pray that you and all God's holy people will have the power to understand the greatness of Christ's love—how wide and how long and how high and how deep that love is. Christ's love is greater than anyone can ever know, but I pray that you will be able to know that love. Then you can be filled with the fullness of God.

EPHESIANS 3:16-19 NCV

This is the ultimate secret of moving toward wholeness:
we love.

DIVINE LOVE ALWAYS LEADS TO WHOLENESS.
Only the love of God is free from all self-serving motivation.
Only His love comes without reservation or condition. We find
in Jesus Christ the only love that makes us truly whole. This is
why ultimately wholeness cannot be defined by our ability to
experience love but by our ability to *exercise* love.

The most basic definition I've used for wholeness is simply
51 percent, where you give more than you take. What if in every
situation you made a commitment to make a greater
contribution than withdrawal—whether financial, relational,
emotional, or the investment of your time? Jesus is our best
example of 100 percent—a person whose entire life was given
to giving. *Jesus always gave more than He took.
He still does.* Everyone who genuinely engages Jesus in a
relationship receives far more than they ever give.

*In the same way, the Son of Man did not come to be served. He came
to serve others and to give his life as a ransom for many people."*

MARK 10:45 NCV

Modern psychiatry is the study of human dysfunction. Its expertise is in identifying, describing, and defining expressions of human brokenness. But the path to wholeness cannot be discovered by concentrating on the signs of fragmentation. This is why Jesus is our best and only hope. Jesus was truly whole. He was a pure expression of a healthy human being. While we can learn about God by studying His divinity, we equally can learn about man by studying His humanity. In Jesus we unlock the mystery of wholeness. *Wholeness is a promise for all of us.* God fully intends to make whole disciples out of broken people. His love unleashed in us is our only hope for the process of wholeness to find its completion.

Love in its purest expression is not something that is received but something that is given. *God is love not because He is most loved but because He is most loving.*

TO PROPERLY PURSUE LOVE, WE MUST STRIVE TO GIVE IT AWAY RATHER THAN SIMPLY FIND IT.

When we consume things, we are materialists. When we consume people, we are cannibals. *In the most dysfunctional of human relationships, we see people as existing for our benefit.* We are so longing for love that every time someone comes close to us, we devour them, oblivious to our selfishness. *We become emotional leeches.* After we've sucked someone dry, we detach and seek our next victim.

Genuine love is never self-motivated (1 Corinthians 13:5). When we open ourselves *to* love, we open ourselves *for* love. We are most whole when we are most free to give. HOLINESS AND WHOLENESS ARE INSEPARABLE.

Jesus answered, "The most important command is this: 'Listen, people of Israel! The Lord our God is the only Lord. Love the Lord your God with all your heart, all your soul, all your mind, and all your strength.' The second command is this: 'Love your neighbor as you love yourself.' There are no commands more important than these."

MARK 12:29-31 NCV

Jesus clearly says your relationships are more important to God than anything else. *You are never closer to the kingdom of God than when relationships are your priority.* First is your relationship to God, and inseparable from this relationship with your Creator are your relationships to others. This is not sequential. It's not love God, then love yourself, then love others; it is love God and love others as you love yourself.

THE MORE OF OURSELVES THAT WE GIVE AWAY, THE MORE WHOLE WE BECOME. THE MORE COMPLETELY WE LOVE, THE MORE COMPLETE LOVE MAKES US.

When Jesus prays for His disciples in John 17, He prays for wholeness. There is no fragmentation in God; love is always the motivation, the intent, and the outcome of the Godhead. *Everything about God is good,* and everything flows from God. He is the eternal giver, the source of every good and perfect gift. We were designed to live this way. *We were created to be expressions of the goodness and wholeness of God.*

CHAPTER EIGHT

THE SUSTAINING
POWER OF BECOMING

We all show the Lord's glory, and we are being changed

to be like him. This change in us brings ever greater

glory, which comes from the Lord, who is the Spirit.

2 CORINTHIANS 3:18 NCV

PERSEVERANCE

is more than just *waiting*.
It's about how and why we wait.
It is the ability to stand and
THRIVE UNDER PRESSURE.

Often we miss the undeniable work of God because we give up too soon. Perseverance is often the only thing that separates failure and success. Life is a gauntlet that requires determination.

Sometimes we should close the chapter on an enterprise, but some things we must never quit. *Projects can be dispensed with; virtues are indispensable.* If we treat who we are as being of the same quality as what we do, we are structured for failure. It's easier to replace a lost wallet than it is to regain our lost integrity.

The wisdom of God comes like a gift, yet it is a gift born out of the womb of perseverance. Wisdom is nurtured and formed in the context of trials and temptations. For wisdom to be forged properly in our hearts, it requires us to stand the pressure cooker of life.

God will give wisdom generously to all who ask, but that promise is preceded by a description of the journey we all must take (James 1:2-5). *Perseverance is the necessary link to wisdom.*

Perseverance has multiple dimensions. In the Scriptures the same word can be translated as "endurance" or even "patience."

WHEN WE HOLD OUT FOR THE GOOD,
OUR PERSEVERANCE IS EXPRESSED AS PATIENCE.

WHEN WE HOLD ON TO THE GOOD,
OUR PERSEVERANCE IS EXPRESSED AS ENDURANCE.

To persevere requires wisdom in the process, and it also grows us in wisdom through the process. When we do not persevere, we do not grow in wisdom. Whenever God places us in circumstances where perseverance is critical, He is trying to birth wisdom in us. When we circumvent the process, it is a miscarriage of wisdom.

Patience ensures that we do not move faster than God. Waiting on God requires that we continue to do what is right even when our situation does not change. *Patience holds out for the good* (2 Peter 3:8-9).

Suffering must not be used as an excuse for impatience (James 5:10-11). Endurance ensures that we do not lose our strength before the task is done. *Endurance holds on to the good.*

Great suffering can accompany a life entirely given to God. *Perseverance is both the resolve to be patient and the commitment to endure.* Perseverance finds the good in the worst of circumstances.

Joy and suffering are bound together in the Scriptures. Suffering is not a virtue; it is a reality. You are not to pursue suffering; suffering certainly will pursue you. *Suffering is not the source of joy, but suffering is not a joyless setting.* Trials are not the source of joy, but trials are where we can find our greatest opportunities for joy. When you belong to God, trials become both a reminder of your need for God and a promise that God will meet you in the midst of it. If God is your greatest pleasure, then trials become your greatest joy. The key to experiencing this ULTIMATE JOY becomes perseverance.

Jesus gives us the best insight into the relationship between suffering and joy. It was not for the joy of the cross that Jesus allowed Himself to be crucified; it was for the joy He could see through the cross (Hebrews 12:2).

Followers of Christ suffer just like everyone else (Romans 5:1-5). The pain is just as real, the disappointment just as deep, the tears just as profound. Yet how we face suffering is quite different. *God allows us to see through the suffering.* We rejoice in our sufferings knowing that our pain is not without meaning. We persevere in the confidence that we ourselves are being transformed. Perseverance produces character, and character, hope. And hope is the ultimate gift gained in wisdom.

God longs to give us wisdom, and it is born out of perseverance. *Only the testing of our faith develops the perseverance we need.* God desires to do some things in our lives that can come no other way except by our walking the path of perseverance. To become like Christ, this ordeal must be faced. You can be filled with joy even in the midst of suffering when you pursue character and not comfort. You can consider trials as the perfect environment for INDESCRIBABLE JOY when you embrace your circumstances as God's incubator to form you in His image.

God allows and at times causes us to go through circumstances that strip away all falsehood and leave us with our real selves. *God's ultimate intent is not to leave us faithless, but to leave us faith-full.* God wants us to have no doubt of the work He has done within us, to know that we have what it takes to walk through fire.

God knows our needs, but sometimes we are oblivious to our need for God. *Trials realign us with reality and position us for divine encounter.* Perseverance is critical so that we don't turn to another source of provision.

The place of our greatest vulnerability is the vacuum created between our need and God's provision. Satan knows God fully intends to supply our every need, so he tempts us to choose another way before God meets us in the middle of the test. He tried to convince Jesus to turn stones into bread (Matthew 4:1-11). The human condition begins to make sense when you realize that **most of us are eating rocks** instead of waiting on God to bring us His bread. We keep trying to meet the deepest longings of our souls apart from the God who intimately created us.

When God tests our faith, the evil one attempts to destroy our faith. While God sends us tests to draw us toward Him, Satan tempts us to draw us away from Him. *We cannot be tested without being tempted.*

Have you ever been told that you're going through trials or facing temptations because you're out of God's will? TRIALS AND TEMPTATIONS ARE NOT THE PUNISHMENT OF GOD, BUT THE PROCESS OF GOD. Yes, sometimes our lives are in ruin and we suffer needlessly as a result of our own foolishness. But we must not assume this is always the case.

Jesus chose to wait on God, His provider. However long He must wait, He would persevere. He would rather be hungry waiting on His Father's timing than to be found eating rocks when the bread came.

Hardship does not require famine of joy or enjoyment. It is in the crucible that we not only discover who we are but more profoundly who Christ is within us (Philippians 4:11-13).

CHAPTER NINE

THE WARRIOR'S HEART

God did not give us a spirit that makes us afraid
but a spirit of power and love and self-control.

2 TIMOTHY 1:7 NCV

God calls you to
dream great dreams and to
have the courage to *live* them.
Great DREAMS require great
COURAGE.

To follow Jesus Christ is to choose to live in His adventure. How in the world could you ever imagine a life of faith that does not require risk? Faith and risk are inseparable. It should not come as a surprise to us then that A LIFE OF FAITH IS A LIFE OF COURAGE. While faith as a noun may be about belief, *having faith is all about action. You cannot walk by faith and live in fear.*

The history of God's people is not a record of God searching for courageous men and women who could handle the tasks but of God transforming the hearts of cowards and calling them to live courageous lives. Adam and Eve hid; Abraham lied; Moses ran; David deceived; Esther wavered; Elijah contemplated suicide; John the Baptist doubted; Peter denied; Judas betrayed. And those are just some of the leading characters.

The Hebrew word RUACH, which normally is translated "spirit," "wind," or "breath," also can be translated "courage." When God breathes His Spirit into us, He not only gives us His power but, more importantly, His courage. When we read Paul's admonition to "be filled with the Spirit" (Ephesians 5:18), we often translate it to mean "be filled with God's power." It would be far more accurate to understand it as "be filled with God's courage." What is the point of having God's power if you lack the courage to actually use it? Only when you embrace God's calling on your life will you need God-inspired courage. *We often ask for God's power to accomplish our small dreams; instead we should cry out for God's courage to step out on His bold adventure.*

Without courage we cannot live the life we choose— instead we choose to relinquish life. We conform to the path of least resistance and abdicate our freedom. So in the end

A LIFE WITHOUT COURAGE IS A LIFE WITHOUT VIRTUE!

EVEN JOSHUA NEEDED A PUSH TO BE BOLD. It was only after the death of Moses that God spoke to Joshua (Joshua 1:1-9). God made Joshua a bold, all-encompassing promise: "I will give you every place where you set your foot." The second promise Joshua received was as revealing as it may have been inspiring: "No one will be able to stand up against you all the days of your life." A promise of conquest, yes, but not a promise of tranquility. Joshua's enemies would not be able to stand against him, but they would try. There would be two sides to the fulfillment of this challenge: GOD'S PART, "I will never leave you nor forsake you," and JOSHUA'S PART, "Be strong and courageous." This command was given to Joshua three times in the same discourse.

It was God's promise, but it was Joshua's responsibility to bring it to pass. The people of Israel saw no dichotomy between *the sacred work of God and the significant role of men and women* to do that work. It was both God and Moses. It would be both God and Joshua. God would lead Joshua, but Joshua would lead Israel.

We seem uncomfortable with this understanding of how God works. We feign humility and without intention we affirm a false belief system. When something bad happens, it obviously was because of you or me, not God. But when something good happens, it's obviously God, not you or me. This demeans the marvelous work of God in the life of an individual.

There's something God wants you to do—not to sit back and watch *Him* do it or passively *wait* for Him to do, but a calling that God waits for *you* to embrace, pursue, and fulfill. *God chooses to entrust His most sacred work to people just like you and me.*

God expected more from Joshua and His people than for them to passively wait for Him to secure the land for them. GOD WOULD GO WITH THEM, BUT HE WOULD NOT GO FOR THEM. The quest would require Joshua to be both a desperate follower of God and an extraordinary leader of men. It is not incidental that God exhorted him to be both strong *and* courageous; Joshua would have to lead the way both in conquest and in character.

There is a difference between momentary courage and moral courage. The first energizes you to rush into a burning building and save a child trapped in a fire. The second empowers you to live a life worthy of being emulated. Both kinds of courage are important.

Whether leading multitudes or just living life, we will find ourselves challenged to sacrifice what is right for what is expedient. *To be strong is to be rooted and defined by what is true.*

God called Joshua to build his life on what He had already said.

> *"Be careful to obey all the law my servant Moses gave you; do not turn from it to the right or to the left, that you may be successful wherever you go. Do not let this Book of the Law depart from your mouth; meditate on it day and night, so that you may be careful to do everything written in it. Then you will be prosperous and successful" (Joshua 1:7-8 NIV).*

Joshua's success first and foremost would depend on the trueness of his moral compass.

How many times have we pointed to not knowing God's will for our lives as the reason we are paralyzed from doing it? Yet, as with Joshua, there is enough truth in the Scriptures to fill our entire lives. The problem is not that we don't know what to do, but that we don't do what we know. THE KEY TO THE FUTURE IS NOT REVELATION, BUT OBEDIENCE. When we submit our lives to what God has made known, the future becomes clearer to us. When we neglect to do what we know, we begin to live as if we were walking through a fog. If we are not careful we will find ourselves condemning God for being silent, when in fact we have condemned ourselves for refusing to listen.

God calls us to live from the inside out. When we live by truth, we establish our integrity. Each "be strong" that God spoke to Joshua was followed by a call to be courageous. God was ordering Joshua not only to hold on to the good but to pursue it with passion. He was to move with urgency and purpose.

Our courage directly affects the speed at which the future unfolds. God loves to do His work through ordinary people like you and me. Even cosmic battles will be won through dust and breath (Romans 16:20).

When we walk in truth, we accelerate the process and literally fast-forward the future. When we remove disobedience from our lives, we are able to respond without hesitation when the moment calls for courage. CRISES RARELY AFFORD US THE LUXURY OF CONTEMPLATION. When courage is fueled by integrity and formed out of humility, it allows us to act without hesitation when the moment requires it. *There is a direct relationship between courage and our ability to respond quickly.*

When God speaks, it requires immediate attention. If you respond to God's call, you will be tested to the very core of your being. God will not save you from the fire but will in fact throw you into it. The promise that He will be with you and never forsake you is *both a promise and a warning.* A divine journey cannot be completed without divine intervention.

COURAGE IS NOT THE ABSENCE OF FEAR; IT IS THE ABSENCE OF SELF. Courage is the highest expression of humility. Courage moves us to risk ourselves for others or for a higher cause. Courage frees us from the fears that would rob us of life itself. It is here that courage and creativity come together. Without courage we become conformists. With courage we once again become the creative beings God designed us to be. The fear of God is not only the beginning of all wisdom but the place of freedom from fear. *When we are free from fear, we are finally free to live.*

"To live is Christ and to die is gain" (Philippians 1:21). God invites us to join Him on the quest for honor, to live a life of genuine courage. *The way is clear: if we would just die, we can begin to live.* This path is one where only dead men can go. Cowards are more than welcome, but you should know up front that how you begin the journey is not how you will finish it. Who you will become will surprise even you.

CHAPTER TEN

THE GENERATIVE SPIRIT

DATE

Disaster Relief

RNIA

*You are rich in everything—in faith,
in speaking, in knowledge, in truly
wanting to help, and in the love you
learned from us. In the same way, be
strong also in the grace of giving.*

2 CORINTHIANS 8:7 NCV

GENEROSITY
is *love in action,*
and love is measured in
GIVING, not taking.

LIFE IS MOST ENJOYED WHEN WE GIVE OURSELVES AWAY. Generous people give more than their things; they genuinely give themselves. In the most marvelous of ways, those who give most freely live most freely.

Generosity is the overflow of love. Love not only expands our heart, but it increases our capacity to give of ourselves. Jesus reminds us, "Greater love has no one than this, that he lay down his life for his friends" (John 15:13 NIV). The apex of generosity is sacrifice. *Generosity isn't about how much we give but about how much it costs us.* Generosity isn't about counting what you've given in comparison to someone else. GENEROSITY IS ABOUT BEING FREE. The generous are free from the things of this world. While they own possessions, their possessions don't own them. Their agenda is to contribute. They are investors, not consumers.

Generosity flows in so many directions. Few investments are as important as our time, and you can never underestimate the importance of being generous with praise. *Generosity creates an environment for emotional health.*

The Scriptures remind us that the greedy stir up dissension (Proverbs 28:25), while the generous foster wholeness. Generosity is motivated by love, but greed is fueled by lust. Greed is narcissistic; generosity is Christlike. *Greed is a product of self-love; generosity is the product of selfless love.* The greatest application of generosity is not financial but relational. Do we treat people as objects to be used or as gifts to be treasured?

JESUS WAS HISTORY'S TRUE INCURABLE ROMANTIC. His life and death are the standard by which all romance should be measured. His was an act of unconditional love; His life, the greatest love story ever told. To want to take is not romantic; to long to give, that's romance. Every writer whose retelling found its way into the pages of Scripture tells the story of Jesus as God's ultimate act of love. With love as God's motive, it should not surprise us that the events of Jesus' life culminated in His ultimate sacrifice. It also should not surprise us that God, who is love, acts with such immeasurable generosity.

Even one wasted life is a tragedy to God. God's intention is to move us out of the paralysis of existence and bring us into a life that is productive and meaningful. We receive God's grace because He is gracious. All who enter the kingdom of heaven must be certain of one thing: Admission is a gift. When you understand the generosity of God, you know that *God finds no pleasure in the death of the wicked*, but in fact finds pleasure when they turn from their ways and live (Ezekiel 18:23; 2 Peter 3:9). You can choose to hold God's generosity against Him, or you can receive the abundance of the life He offers.

GOD LOVES TO POUR HIS GIFTS UPON HIS CHILDREN. The Scriptures are resplendent with promises of blessing from God to His people (2 Peter 1:17). When we live in a proper relationship with God, it has a dramatic effect on every area of our lives. The Scriptures tell us that God desires to bless our relationships, our marriages, our children, our work, our finances, and our very lives.

The more good we do, the more good we are able to do. *Generosity increases our capacity to bless others.* When generosity is unleashed, it flows to every area of our lives. We become generous not only with our money but also with our time, effort, gifts, talents, passions, every part of us. When you choose to live generously, you can know that "you will be made rich in every way so that you can be generous on every occasion" (2 Corinthians 9:11 NIV).

There's nothing wrong with having wealth. God richly provides us with everything for our enjoyment. God wants us to enjoy our lives. He finds pleasure in our pleasure. Jesus did not call His disciples to reject a life of affluence and embrace a life of poverty. He simply called them to follow Him, to reject a life of greed and embrace a life of generosity. *God will hold us accountable not just for the gifts we use, but for those we neglect.* When we embrace prosperity as a gift from God entrusted to us for the good of many, we are laying up for ourselves treasures in heaven, not born out of greed, but born out of the very heart of God.

THE GENEROUS SEE THEMSELVES AS STEWARDS OF GOD'S TREASURES. They are not cautious in giving themselves away, for God Himself is their source of replenishment. They understand everything to be the Lord's and thus are free to give without reservation. It's not that they give carelessly or without thoughtfulness, nor is it that they give without consideration of need. They are the contributors of life. *They are the true investors in the human spirit.* Wherever they are, there is more. They never leave a place or a relationship having taken more than they have given. Yet somehow they never leave empty. In giving, they find themselves enriched. They are anomalies in the human economy.

THE TAKERS OF THIS WORLD ALWAYS NEED MORE. They are always hungry, always craving. THE GIVERS ARE UNEXPLAINABLY FULL. Those who refuse to believe in God's economy never understand the endless flow of their resources. The takers are always looking for happiness, convinced somehow that the next thing they grab will be their source of joy.

The giver is always open-handed, yet never empty-handed. The generous have found the secret to happiness. They have found the joy of living through serving others. *When we become generous, we become like God.* Every creative act of God is created not out of selfishness or self-indulgence, but out of His generosity. We demean the nature of our God-given creativity when we use it for anything beneath His character. Creativity and generosity are to be identical sisters, always expressing and resulting in a work of beauty. Greed and ungratefulness caustically make nothing out of something; generosity and gratitude creatively make something out of nothing (see Ephesians 4:28).

Grace is never less than the law. GRACE IS NOT FREEDOM TO LIVE BENEATH THE LAW, BUT TO LIVE BEYOND THE LAW.

CHAPTER ELEVEN

THE DIVINE IMAGINATION

Wisdom is like a woman shouting in the street;

she raises her voice in the city squares.

She cries out in the noisy street

and shouts at the city gates:

"You fools, how long will you be foolish?

How long will you make fun of wisdom

and hate knowledge?

If only you had listened when I corrected you,

I would have told you what's in my heart;

I would have told you what I am thinking.

PROVERBS 1:20-23 NCV

When you

FEAR GOD

and nothing else,

you discover the

freedom to *pursue*

great adventure.

God calls you to a life that cannot be lived without wisdom. *While many of us long for God to give us a map so that we can simply follow it, He instead gives us a compass that points the way.* What we continually ask for is to know God's will for our lives; what God continually offers us is His wisdom for our lives. So critical is wisdom to the journey that God offers it as a gift to all who would desire it (James 1:5).

The heart of a fool is motivated by personal gain. The heart of wisdom is motivated by the good of others. While wisdom does not always guarantee a life of riches and honor, *wisdom always produces a rich and honorable life.*

WISDOM CREATES AND PRODUCES GOOD. Wisdom not only sees the good that must be done now, but it catalyzes such events that result in a good future. Wherever wisdom flows, good follows. Not everything that happens *to* a person who lives wisely is good, but everything that happens *from* a person who lives wisely is good. This doesn't mean that walking in wisdom is painless, but the ultimate results of wisdom are health, freedom, and creativity.

One can be highly educated and also be wise, but it is not a given. You can be uneducated from a conventional standard and still be a person of great wisdom. The converse is also true. You can accomplish great things in the academic world and live a life of foolishness.

Wisdom always finds a way through the mess we make of life. It doesn't find the easiest way, but the way marked by the footprints of God. Wisdom is the product of SACRED IMAGINATION. Wisdom knows the way to freedom. Where there is wisdom, there is always HOPE. Wisdom simplifies. Wisdom clarifies. Wisdom untangles. Wisdom unshackles. Wisdom illuminates. WISDOM LIBERATES. In the end, wisdom enlightens us to live lives of nobility.

Wisdom is more than simply the ability to *see beyond* ourselves, but even perhaps more profoundly, to *see within* ourselves. Wisdom is the ability to cut to the core of complex issues. Wisdom not only allows us to move beyond living a senseless life; it helps us begin to *make sense of life.* The fool acts without reflection; the wise man reflects on his actions.

Wisdom becomes the ability to see choice as cause and consequence and benefit as effect. When we see our circumstances as isolated from our actions, we abdicate personal responsibility for our lives. Taken to an extreme, we hold God accountable for the consequences of our actions and become embittered toward Him. It's as if we want the freedom to make choices but expect God to make sure that we don't have to live with the consequences of our choices.

At times we would rather believe in luck than in responsibility, but superstition is nothing more than an improper connection between CAUSE AND EFFECT.

When we disconnect our circumstances from our choices, we choose to live powerless lives. When we embrace the interconnection between our present decisions and our future opportunities, we regain the power to set our course and to shape our journey. A proper view of cause and effect grows us in wisdom, and brings *greater freedom* to our lives.

Wisdom refuses to surrender the freedom of the future for a temporary indulgence. Wisdom recognizes that while some opportunities are captivating, beneath the surface they are ready to take you captive. Wisdom recognizes that the inseparable relationship between cause and effect is more than a natural phenomenon; it is a spiritual reality.

Do not be fooled: You cannot cheat God. People harvest only what they plant. If they plant to satisfy their sinful selves, their sinful selves will bring them ruin. But if they plant to please the Spirit, they will receive eternal life from the Spirit. We must not become tired of doing good. We will receive our harvest of eternal life at the right time if we do not give up. When we have the opportunity to help anyone, we should do it. But we should give special attention to those who are in the family of believers.
GALATIANS 6:7-10 NCV

Whether the language is sowing and reaping, cause and effect, a contemporary understanding of good and bad karma, or simply understanding that what goes around comes around, *wisdom begins at connecting the dots between the quality of our decisions and the quality of our lives.*

The future is the sum total of all the choices that are made in the present and in the past. Fortunately, that sum total includes the choices made by God. A significant aspect of wisdom is having a future orientation. Wisdom gives us a perspective that always looks toward the future from the present and always looks from the future to the present.

From the vantage point of the fool, the world appears to exist in isolated units. The connection between the absentee father and the promiscuous daughter remains undetected. The relationship between bitterness toward your parents and coldness toward your children is unperceived. The repercussions of extramarital infidelity are never linked to premarital promiscuity. Debt remains unconnected to greed; violence remains unconnected to hate; the loss of hope remains disconnected from the loss of faith.

Wisdom sees everything in life as interconnected. Wisdom does not allow us to stand apart from the rest of the world.

WISDOM SEES ALL LIFE THROUGH RELATIONSHIPS—
our relationships to God, to others, to nature, and more. It is
recognizing that our best selves can only be discovered when
we consider others above ourselves.

Over the generations, wisdom has become more about ideas
than living. Philosophy is literally the love of wisdom, but little
of wisdom's original essence is left in that discipline. It is so
much easier to escape to Walden Pond and contemplate life than
it is to *return from it and really live.* Wisdom frees us
from living disconnected lives. *Wisdom frees us* from superstitions
that constrain us and broken relationships that cripple us.

WISDOM TRANSFORMS THE WAY WE SEE REALITY. It
sees no distinction between the physical and the spiritual. God
created the material universe, and He declared it good. Even in a
fallen world, wisdom sees the good that will come through choices
made. This distinct view of reality known as wisdom is nothing
less than seeing life from God's vantage point. THE EPICENTER
OF ALL WISDOM IS GOD HIMSELF.

The Scriptures remind us that the fear of the Lord is the beginning of all wisdom. Then what exactly does this mean? *When we fear God, we fear nothing else.* It is only in the fear of God that we find ourselves free from the fear of death, of failure, and all the other fears that bind us.

When the fear of God is absent from our lives, we become slaves to lesser fears, and *your fears define the boundaries of your life.* When you fear God, you are subject only to Him. You align yourself to love and truth. You are never afraid to love or forgive when you fear God. You are never afraid to do good when you fear God. You are never afraid to face the truth or speak the truth when you fear God. You live with a calm assurance that in all these things God finds great pleasure.

The fear of God is the beginning of wisdom, for only in this place are we forced to face ourselves and see ourselves for who we really are. When you are a follower of Jesus Christ, you are committed to follow the truth wherever it leads you. This fear of God frees you to risk, to fail, to dream, to attempt great things.

When you fear God, you understand that you have come to Him in a condition of sinfulness. You know God as not only a God of holiness but also a God of infinite compassion. You live with the knowledge of His grace. You bask in the promise that if you confess your sin, He is faithful and just to forgive you of all your sin and to cleanse you from all unrighteousness (1 John 1:9).

It is only in the fear of God that we are truly free. *We see God for who He really is.* We see ourselves for who we really are. We understand the condition of the world in which we live. And we are ENLIGHTENED to see a world—or should I say *kingdom*—that waits to come. Wisdom understands the heart of God. The woman of wisdom, the man who is wise, such people embrace that heart and live by it. Only here are we truly free.

CHAPTER TWELVE

THE GREATNESS OF SERVANTHOOD

Train yourself to serve God . . .serving God helps
you in every way by bringing you blessings in this
life and in the future life, too.

1 TIMOTHY 4:7-8 NCV

SERVANTHOOD

is not God's way to get us to the

place where we will only be served;

it is both the WAY *and*

the LIFE of the kingdom of God.

Jesus is without ambiguity when He tells us that He is the way, the truth, and the life and that no one comes to the Father except by Him (John 14:6). *His invitation is to join an uprising. If we choose to follow Him, there will be within us a revolution of the soul.* He will do nothing less than translate us from a kingdom of emptiness into His kingdom where we will begin to live in a new reality.

THE WAY OF GOD IS THE PATH OF SERVANTHOOD. THIS IS NOT A TEST TO SEE IF WE DESERVE BETTER. IT IS GOD OFFERING US THE BEST OF HIMSELF AND THE BEST OF LIFE. GOD CALLS US TO BE SERVANTS BECAUSE GOD IS A SERVANT.

God stands alone as Creator and Redeemer. He also stands there as Servant. He created us to be creative. He invites us to reconcile men to Himself. He also calls us to choose the path of servanthood. *This is not about* RELIGION; *it is about* REVOLUTION (Galatians 5:1-6).

On this journey we discover that not only does humility lead to integrity and integrity lead to courage, that gratitude leads to wholeness, which results in generosity, but we also will discover that faithfulness develops perseverance, which grows us in wisdom.

As we grow in humility, gratitude, and faithfulness, we find ourselves with the strength of character to endure the greatest hardships and overcome our greatest challenges. Our capacity to be resilient will increase as we journey deeper into these virtues. When we are resilient, we have an unexplainable *capacity to recover* from illness, adversity, and even depression.

As we grow in integrity, wholeness, and perseverance, we find integration in our lives. *In a world filled with brokenness, the capacity to integrate all the pieces is critical for health.* This is part of God's promise in the work of transformation.

THE ULTIMATE END OF CHARACTER TRANSFORMATION IS NOT FREEDOM FROM SIN, BUT FREEDOM TO ONCE AGAIN BE ALL THAT GOD DESIGNED FOR US TO BE.

As we grow in generosity, we become generative and creative in our contributions to the good of others. When we walk in the wisdom of God, we see the hidden possibilities and opportunities missed by so many others. *Wisdom always finds a way.* It is the fountain of intellectual creativity and innovation.

When we fear God, we find the freedom and the courage to pursue dreams far too big for ourselves, yet courage is the only hope for great dreams. It is here where the synergistic interplay of courage, wisdom, and generosity make us most creative. Once again, GOD'S GIFT TO US IS HIMSELF.

The character of God, the beauty of His personhood, the expression of His goodness, He longs to share with us. What would the world look like, what would we look like, if we became like Him? The One who wrapped a towel around His waist and washed His disciples' feet invites us to become like Him in His servanthood. This is *the ultimate destination,* to become the person God dreams of and to share those dreams with others.

My brothers and sisters, God called you to be free, but do not use your freedom as an excuse to do what pleases your sinful self. Serve each other with love. The whole law is made complete in this one command: "Love your neighbor as you love yourself."

GALATIANS 5:13-14 NCV

ABOUT THE AUTHOR

ERWIN RAPHAEL McMANUS

serves as lead pastor and cultural architect of
Mosaic in Los Angeles, California. From the global
center of change, Mosaic emerges as a reference point
for the future church. As founder of Awaken, Erwin
collaborates with a team of dreamers and innovators who
specialize in the field of developing and unleashing personal
and organizational creativity. As a national and international
consultant his expertise focuses on culture, change, leadership,
and creativity. He partners with Bethel Theological Seminary
as distinguished professor and futurist. Erwin's first book, *An
Unstoppable Force*, was a 2002 ECPA Gold Medallion Award finalist.
He is also author of *Seizing Your Divine Moment* and *Uprising:
A Revolution of the Soul*, which was the featured book and theme
for the 2004 Promise Keepers conferences. He and his
wife, Kim, have two children, Aaron and Mariah,
and a daughter in the Lord, Paty.

www.awakenhumanity.org
www.erwinmcmanus.com